D1827564

BIBLICAL
THEOLOGY
WORKBOOK

BY

A WRITER AND THE WORD

Table of Contents

Why Biblical Theology?

Biblical Theology is a branch of Biblical Studies which seeks to explain the whole story of Scripture and understand various aspects of theology within the unfolding narrative of Scripture itself. Biblical Theology takes what the Bible says within the Bible's own context and development.

Biblical Theology is often pitted against Systematic Theology. However, the two actually work hand in hand. Biblical Theology explores Scripture through time, whereas Systematic Theology explores Scripture without reference to time. Biblical Theology follows the narrative flow, while Systematic Theology stands above the whole. Biblical Theology seeks the redemptive-narrative of the Bible, while Systematic Theology seeks Doctrines and Dogmas.

Biblical Theology begins with the text. We begin with exegesis, historical context, and literary genre. The priority is to understand the Bible on its own terms, and then to trace God's unfolding revelation as it progresses.

Two major approaches develop. The first I'll call *centric*, and the second *thematic*. The Centric approach seeks to find a *central* theme that can uphold the whole of Scripture. For instance, James Hamilton sees the central biblical-theological focus of Scripture as "God's glory in salvation through judgment." GK Beale sees the central theme of Scripture as revolving around "Creation and Recreation." Stephen Wellum and Peter Gentry disagree with both these approaches, and rather see the central backbone to Scripture's narrative as "Kingdom through Covenant." However, it gets parsed out, these theologians are searching for a Biblical-Theological approach that uncovers the central theme of Scripture.

The second approach is more *thematic*. Rather than seeking a center, this approach takes on the various themes that Scripture contains. For instance, we could trace the theme of *presence* throughout Scripture's grand meta-narrative, starting in Genesis, moving to Exodus and the Tabernacle, through the history books and the Temple, and right up to the Incarnation, culminating in Revelation with the consummation of God's presence. Doing this isn't arguing for *presence* as the central theme, but rather a theme. There are tons of various thematic approaches to Scripture. You can see Appendix A for a list of potential themes, or Appendix C for a list of thematic biblical-theological books.

The goal of this book is to provide a simple frame of reference for you to study the various themes and centers of Biblical Theology. This book is built so that you can take *any* theme in Scripture and work out all the various developments across the biblical storyline.

How to Use This Book

You may not know where to start, so let me help you.
If you flip to the back of this book, you'll find three appendices. The first (Appendix A) is a list of thematic biblical theological themes, like presence, kingdom, and sonship. These are all ideas to help jumpstart your thinking. You can pick one of these themes to start with or you can pick your own. However, this list is not exhaustive. It is merely a springboard for you to get started.

I've also included in Appendix B a list of introductory books. These books aren't necessarily *doing* biblical theology, they're exploring what biblical theology is and *how* to do it. If you're new to biblical theology as a discipline, then I would suggest picking one of these books up to get you started.

In Appendix C I've compiled a short list of thematic and centric biblical theologies that actually do biblical theology. They trace themes, draw conclusions, and get deep into the exegesis of texts. These are great resources to work through with this workbook. There's a ton of resources out there, some more accessible than others. The importance is that you allow whatever resource you use to bring you back to the biblical text.

Anyway, that's a big picture look at how to use this book. Now let's get a little more practical.

How to Really Use This Book

Once you get the idea of this workbook, the rest is quite simple (difficult, but simple).

At the top of each template is a place to write in the *Theme* you're working through. Let's say you want to work through "Image of God".

Next, you'll actually work through the second page, "Metanarrative Developments and Exegetical Analysis". On this page, you'll work through all the key biblical texts, drawing together a scope of "Image of God" across the grand narrative of Scripture, but also considering each text in its own context (i.e. don't neglect the exegesis of each text). For instance, with "image of God" I would first work through Genesis 1:26-27, and then trace its development through the rest of Scripture.

Once you work through a general overview of the theme, we can move back to the first page and begin to work through a comprehensive definition. Take into account the results of the entire development of your theme.

Next, you'll identify the Major Developments, any typological themes, and fulfillment for that specific theme. A Major Development in image would include the Fall in Genesis 3, Psalm 8, ideas of sonship in 2 Samuel 7 and Psalm 2, as well as developments in Jesus and Paul's thought.

From there, you'll have a good understanding of how these texts and thoughts are relevant to life. What's the pastoral application? Why is "image of God" relevant to Christian life, especially in light of its biblical theological development.

And lastly, there's a section to indicate which books and resources you consulted in studying.

One of the things you'll quickly realize is that there's not enough space to do all the work you'll want to. This is merely a primer and springboard for your thoughts and notes. You won't be able to detail out a full exegesis of every passage. The purpose of this book is to give you a starting point.

Now, let's get started. :)

Actually, one last thing.

If you have any questions or feedback, you can reach me on Instagram at @awriterandtheword.

BIBLICAL
THEOLOGY
WORKBOOK

Biblical Theological Theme:

Definition:

Major Developments, Typology, Fulfillment:

Relevance and Application:

Books, Resources, Reference Material:

Metanarrative Developments and Exegetical Analysis:

Pentateuch:

History:

Wisdom:

Prophets:

Gospels:

Letters:

Biblical Theological Theme:

Definition:

Major Developments, Typology, Fulfillment:

Relevance and Application:

Books, Resources, Reference Material:

Metanarrative Developments and Exegetical Analysis:

Pentateuch:

History:

Wisdom:

Prophets:

Gospels:

Letters:

Biblical Theological Theme:

Definition:

Major Developments, Typology, Fulfillment:

Relevance and Application:

Books, Resources, Reference Material:

Metanarrative Developments and Exegetical Analysis:

Pentateuch:

History:

Wisdom:

Prophets:

Gospels:

Letters:

Biblical Theological Theme:

Definition:

Major Developments, Typology, Fulfillment:

Relevance and Application:

Books, Resources, Reference Material:

Metanarrative Developments and Exegetical Analysis:

Pentateuch:

History:

Wisdom:

Prophets:

Gospels:

Letters:

Biblical Theological Theme:

Definition:

Major Developments, Typology, Fulfillment:

Relevance and Application:

Books, Resources, Reference Material:

Metanarrative Developments and Exegetical Analysis:

Pentateuch:

History:

Wisdom:

Prophets:

Gospels:

Letters:

Biblical Theological Theme:

Definition:

Major Developments, Typology, Fulfillment:

Relevance and Application:

Books, Resources, Reference Material:

Metanarrative Developments and Exegetical Analysis:

Pentateuch:

History:

Wisdom:

Prophets:

Gospels:

Letters:

Biblical Theological Theme:

Definition:

Major Developments, Typology, Fulfillment:

Relevance and Application:

Books, Resources, Reference Material:

Metanarrative Developments and Exegetical Analysis:

Pentateuch:

History:

Wisdom:

Prophets:

Gospels:

Letters:

Biblical Theological Theme:

Definition:

Major Developments, Typology, Fulfillment:

Relevance and Application:

Books, Resources, Reference Material:

Metanarrative Developments and Exegetical Analysis:

Pentateuch:

History:

Wisdom:

Prophets:

Gospels:

Letters:

Biblical Theological Theme:

Definition:

Major Developments, Typology, Fulfillment:

Relevance and Application:

Books, Resources, Reference Material:

Metanarrative Developments and Exegetical Analysis:

Pentateuch:

History:

Wisdom:

Prophets:

Gospels:

Letters:

Biblical Theological Theme:

Definition:

Major Developments, Typology, Fulfillment:

Relevance and Application:

Books, Resources, Reference Material:

Metanarrative Developments and Exegetical Analysis:

Pentateuch:

History:

Wisdom:

Prophets:

Gospels:

Letters:

Biblical Theological Theme:

Definition:

Major Developments, Typology, Fulfillment:

Relevance and Application:

Books, Resources, Reference Material:

Metanarrative Developments and Exegetical Analysis:

Pentateuch:

History:

Wisdom:

Prophets:

Gospels:

Letters:

Biblical Theological Theme:

Definition:

Major Developments, Typology, Fulfillment:

Relevance and Application:

Books, Resources, Reference Material:

Metanarrative Developments and Exegetical Analysis:

Pentateuch:

History:

Wisdom:

Prophets:

Gospels:

Letters:

Biblical Theological Theme:

Definition:

Major Developments, Typology, Fulfillment:

Relevance and Application:

Books, Resources, Reference Material:

Metanarrative Developments and Exegetical Analysis:

Pentateuch:

History:

Wisdom:

Prophets:

Gospels:

Letters:

Biblical Theological Theme:

Definition:

Major Developments, Typology, Fulfillment:

Relevance and Application:

Books, Resources, Reference Material:

Metanarrative Developments and Exegetical Analysis:

Pentateuch:

History:

Wisdom:

Prophets:

Gospels:

Letters:

Biblical Theological Theme:

Definition:

Major Developments, Typology, Fulfillment:

Relevance and Application:

Books, Resources, Reference Material:

Metanarrative Developments and Exegetical Analysis:

Pentateuch:

History:

Wisdom:

Prophets:

Gospels:

Letters:

Biblical Theological Theme:

Definition:

Major Developments, Typology, Fulfillment:

Relevance and Application:

Books, Resources, Reference Material:

Metanarrative Developments and Exegetical Analysis:

Pentateuch:

History:

Wisdom:

Prophets:

Gospels:

Letters:

Biblical Theological Theme:

Definition:

Major Developments, Typology, Fulfillment:

Relevance and Application:

Books, Resources, Reference Material:

Metanarrative Developments and Exegetical Analysis:

Pentateuch:

History:

Wisdom:

Prophets:

Gospels:

Letters:

Biblical Theological Theme:

Definition:

Major Developments, Typology, Fulfillment:

Relevance and Application:

Books, Resources, Reference Material:

Metanarrative Developments and Exegetical Analysis:

Pentateuch:

History:

Wisdom:

Prophets:

Gospels:

Letters:

Biblical Theological Theme:

Definition:

Major Developments, Typology, Fulfillment:

Relevance and Application:

Books, Resources, Reference Material:

Metanarrative Developments and Exegetical Analysis:

Pentateuch:

History:

Wisdom:

Prophets:

Gospels:

Letters:

Biblical Theological Theme:

Definition:

Major Developments, Typology, Fulfillment:

Relevance and Application:

Books, Resources, Reference Material:

Metanarrative Developments and Exegetical Analysis:

Pentateuch:

History:

Wisdom:

Prophets:

Gospels:

Letters:

Biblical Theological Theme:

Definition:

Major Developments, Typology, Fulfillment:

Relevance and Application:

Books, Resources, Reference Material:

Metanarrative Developments and Exegetical Analysis:

Pentateuch:

History:

Wisdom:

Prophets:

Gospels:

Letters:

Biblical Theological Theme:

Definition:

Major Developments, Typology, Fulfillment:

Relevance and Application:

Books, Resources, Reference Material:

Metanarrative Developments and Exegetical Analysis:

Pentateuch:

History:

Wisdom:

Prophets:

Gospels:

Letters:

Biblical Theological Theme:

Definition:

Major Developments, Typology, Fulfillment:

Relevance and Application:

Books, Resources, Reference Material:

Metanarrative Developments and Exegetical Analysis:

Pentateuch:

History:

Wisdom:

Prophets:

Gospels:

Letters:

Biblical Theological Theme:

Definition:

Major Developments, Typology, Fulfillment:

Relevance and Application:

Books, Resources, Reference Material:

Metanarrative Developments and Exegetical Analysis:

Pentateuch:

History:

Wisdom:

Prophets:

Gospels:

Letters:

Biblical Theological Theme:

Definition:

Major Developments, Typology, Fulfillment:

Relevance and Application:

Books, Resources, Reference Material:

Metanarrative Developments and Exegetical Analysis:

Pentateuch:

History:

Wisdom:

Prophets:

Gospels:

Letters:

Biblical Theological Theme:

Definition:

Major Developments, Typology, Fulfillment:

Relevance and Application:

Books, Resources, Reference Material:

Metanarrative Developments and Exegetical Analysis:

Pentateuch:

History:

Wisdom:

Prophets:

Gospels:

Letters:

Biblical Theological Theme:

Definition:

Major Developments, Typology, Fulfillment:

Relevance and Application:

Books, Resources, Reference Material:

Metanarrative Developments and Exegetical Analysis:

Pentateuch:

History:

Wisdom:

Prophets:

Gospels:

Letters:

Biblical Theological Theme:

Definition:

Major Developments, Typology, Fulfillment:

Relevance and Application:

Books, Resources, Reference Material:

Metanarrative Developments and Exegetical Analysis:

Pentateuch:

History:

Wisdom:

Prophets:

Gospels:

Letters:

Biblical Theological Theme:

Definition:

Major Developments, Typology, Fulfillment:

Relevance and Application:

Books, Resources, Reference Material:

Metanarrative Developments and Exegetical Analysis:

Pentateuch:

History:

Wisdom:

Prophets:

Gospels:

Letters:

Biblical Theological Theme:

Definition:

Major Developments, Typology, Fulfillment:

Relevance and Application:

Books, Resources, Reference Material:

Metanarrative Developments and Exegetical Analysis:

Pentateuch:

History:

Wisdom:

Prophets:

Gospels:

Letters:

Biblical Theological Theme:

Definition:

Major Developments, Typology, Fulfillment:

Relevance and Application:

Books, Resources, Reference Material:

Metanarrative Developments and Exegetical Analysis:

Pentateuch:

History:

Wisdom:

Prophets:

Gospels:

Letters:

Biblical Theological Theme:

Definition:

Major Developments, Typology, Fulfillment:

Relevance and Application:

Books, Resources, Reference Material:

Metanarrative Developments and Exegetical Analysis:

Pentateuch:

History:

Wisdom:

Prophets:

Gospels:

Letters:

Biblical Theological Theme:

Definition:

Major Developments, Typology, Fulfillment:

Relevance and Application:

Books, Resources, Reference Material:

Metanarrative Developments and Exegetical Analysis:

Pentateuch:

History:

Wisdom:

Prophets:

Gospels:

Letters:

Biblical Theological Theme:

Definition:

Major Developments, Typology, Fulfillment:

Relevance and Application:

Books, Resources, Reference Material:

Metanarrative Developments and Exegetical Analysis:

Pentateuch:

History:

Wisdom:

Prophets:

Gospels:

Letters:

Biblical Theological Theme:

Definition:

Major Developments, Typology, Fulfillment:

Relevance and Application:

Books, Resources, Reference Material:

Metanarrative Developments and Exegetical Analysis:

Pentateuch:

History:

Wisdom:

Prophets:

Gospels:

Letters:

Biblical Theological Theme:

Definition:

Major Developments, Typology, Fulfillment:

Relevance and Application:

Books, Resources, Reference Material:

Metanarrative Developments and Exegetical Analysis:

Pentateuch:

History:

Wisdom:

Prophets:

Gospels:

Letters:

Biblical Theological Theme:

Definition:

Major Developments, Typology, Fulfillment:

Relevance and Application:

Books, Resources, Reference Material:

Metanarrative Developments and Exegetical Analysis:

Pentateuch:

History:

Wisdom:

Prophets:

Gospels:

Letters:

Biblical Theological Theme:

Definition:

Major Developments, Typology, Fulfillment:

Relevance and Application:

Books, Resources, Reference Material:

Metanarrative Developments and Exegetical Analysis:

Pentateuch:

History:

Wisdom:

Prophets:

Gospels:

Letters:

Biblical Theological Theme:

Definition:

Major Developments, Typology, Fulfillment:

Relevance and Application:

Books, Resources, Reference Material:

Metanarrative Developments and Exegetical Analysis:

Pentateuch:

History:

Wisdom:

Prophets:

Gospels:

Letters:

Biblical Theological Theme:

Definition:

Major Developments, Typology, Fulfillment:

Relevance and Application:

Books, Resources, Reference Material:

Metanarrative Developments and Exegetical Analysis:

Pentateuch:

History:

Wisdom:

Prophets:

Gospels:

Letters:

Biblical Theological Theme:

Definition:

Major Developments, Typology, Fulfillment:

Relevance and Application:

Books, Resources, Reference Material:

Metanarrative Developments and Exegetical Analysis:

Pentateuch:

History:

Wisdom:

Prophets:

Gospels:

Letters:

Biblical Theological Theme:

Definition:

Major Developments, Typology, Fulfillment:

Relevance and Application:

Books, Resources, Reference Material:

Metanarrative Developments and Exegetical Analysis:

Pentateuch:

History:

Wisdom:

Prophets:

Gospels:

Letters:

Biblical Theological Theme:

Definition:

Major Developments, Typology, Fulfillment:

Relevance and Application:

Books, Resources, Reference Material:

Metanarrative Developments and Exegetical Analysis:

Pentateuch:

History:

Wisdom:

Prophets:

Gospels:

Letters:

Biblical Theological Theme:

Definition:

Major Developments, Typology, Fulfillment:

Relevance and Application:

Books, Resources, Reference Material:

Metanarrative Developments and Exegetical Analysis:

Pentateuch:

History:

Wisdom:

Prophets:

Gospels:

Letters:

Biblical Theological Theme:

Definition:

Major Developments, Typology, Fulfillment:

Relevance and Application:

Books, Resources, Reference Material:

Metanarrative Developments and Exegetical Analysis:

Pentateuch:

History:

Wisdom:

Prophets:

Gospels:

Letters:

Biblical Theological Theme:

Definition:

Major Developments, Typology, Fulfillment:

Relevance and Application:

Books, Resources, Reference Material:

Metanarrative Developments and Exegetical Analysis:

Pentateuch:

History:

Wisdom:

Prophets:

Gospels:

Letters:

Biblical Theological Theme:

Definition:

Major Developments, Typology, Fulfillment:

Relevance and Application:

Books, Resources, Reference Material:

Metanarrative Developments and Exegetical Analysis:

Pentateuch:

History:

Wisdom:

Prophets:

Gospels:

Letters:

Biblical Theological Theme:

Definition:

Major Developments, Typology, Fulfillment:

Relevance and Application:

Books, Resources, Reference Material:

Metanarrative Developments and Exegetical Analysis:

Pentateuch:

History:

Wisdom:

Prophets:

Gospels:

Letters:

Biblical Theological Theme:

Definition:

Major Developments, Typology, Fulfillment:

Relevance and Application:

Books, Resources, Reference Material:

Metanarrative Developments and Exegetical Analysis:

Pentateuch:

History:

Wisdom:

Prophets:

Gospels:

Letters:

Biblical Theological Theme:

Definition:

Major Developments, Typology, Fulfillment:

Relevance and Application:

Books, Resources, Reference Material:

Metanarrative Developments and Exegetical Analysis:

Pentateuch:

History:

Wisdom:

Prophets:

Gospels:

Letters:

Biblical Theological Theme:

Definition:

Major Developments, Typology, Fulfillment:

Relevance and Application:

Books, Resources, Reference Material:

Metanarrative Developments and Exegetical Analysis:

Pentateuch:

History:

Wisdom:

Prophets:

Gospels:

Letters:

Biblical Theological Theme:

Definition:

Major Developments, Typology, Fulfillment:

Relevance and Application:

Books, Resources, Reference Material:

Metanarrative Developments and Exegetical Analysis:

Pentateuch:

History:

Wisdom:

Prophets:

Gospels:

Letters:

Biblical Theological Theme:

Definition:

Major Developments, Typology, Fulfillment:

Relevance and Application:

Books, Resources, Reference Material:

Metanarrative Developments and Exegetical Analysis:

Pentateuch:

History:

Wisdom:

Prophets:

Gospels:

Letters:

Biblical Theological Theme:

Definition:

Major Developments, Typology, Fulfillment:

Relevance and Application:

Books, Resources, Reference Material:

Metanarrative Developments and Exegetical Analysis:

Pentateuch:

History:

Wisdom:

Prophets:

Gospels:

Letters:

Biblical Theological Theme:

Definition:

Major Developments, Typology, Fulfillment:

Relevance and Application:

Books, Resources, Reference Material:

Metanarrative Developments and Exegetical Analysis:

Pentateuch:

History:

Wisdom:

Prophets:

Gospels:

Letters:

Biblical Theological Theme:

Definition:

Major Developments, Typology, Fulfillment:

Relevance and Application:

Books, Resources, Reference Material:

Metanarrative Developments and Exegetical Analysis:

Pentateuch:

History:

Wisdom:

Prophets:

Gospels:

Letters:

Biblical Theological Theme:

Definition:

Major Developments, Typology, Fulfillment:

Relevance and Application:

Books, Resources, Reference Material:

Metanarrative Developments and Exegetical Analysis:

Pentateuch:

History:

Wisdom:

Prophets:

Gospels:

Letters:

Biblical Theological Theme:

Definition:

Major Developments, Typology, Fulfillment:

Relevance and Application:

Books, Resources, Reference Material:

Metanarrative Developments and Exegetical Analysis:

Pentateuch:

History:

Wisdom:

Prophets:

Gospels:

Letters:

Biblical Theological Theme:

Definition:

Major Developments, Typology, Fulfillment:

Relevance and Application:

Books, Resources, Reference Material:

Metanarrative Developments and Exegetical Analysis:

Pentateuch:

History:

Wisdom:

Prophets:

Gospels:

Letters:

Biblical Theological Theme:

Definition:

Major Developments, Typology, Fulfillment:

Relevance and Application:

Books, Resources, Reference Material:

Metanarrative Developments and Exegetical Analysis:

Pentateuch:

History:

Wisdom:

Prophets:

Gospels:

Letters:

Biblical Theological Theme:

Definition:

Major Developments, Typology, Fulfillment:

Relevance and Application:

Books, Resources, Reference Material:

Metanarrative Developments and Exegetical Analysis:

Pentateuch:

History:

Wisdom:

Prophets:

Gospels:

Letters:

Biblical Theological Theme:

Definition:

Major Developments, Typology, Fulfillment:

Relevance and Application:

Books, Resources, Reference Material:

Metanarrative Developments and Exegetical Analysis:

Pentateuch:

History:

Wisdom:

Prophets:

Gospels:

Letters:

Biblical Theological Theme:

Definition:

Major Developments, Typology, Fulfillment:

Relevance and Application:

Books, Resources, Reference Material:

Metanarrative Developments and Exegetical Analysis:

Pentateuch:

History:

Wisdom:

Prophets:

Gospels:

Letters:

Biblical Theological Theme:

Definition:

Major Developments, Typology, Fulfillment:

Relevance and Application:

Books, Resources, Reference Material:

Metanarrative Developments and Exegetical Analysis:

Pentateuch:

History:

Wisdom:

Prophets:

Gospels:

Letters:

Biblical Theological Theme:

Definition:

Major Developments, Typology, Fulfillment:

Relevance and Application:

Books, Resources, Reference Material:

Metanarrative Developments and Exegetical Analysis:

Pentateuch:

History:

Wisdom:

Prophets:

Gospels:

Letters:

Biblical Theological Theme:

Definition:

Major Developments, Typology, Fulfillment:

Relevance and Application:

Books, Resources, Reference Material:

Metanarrative Developments and Exegetical Analysis:

Pentateuch:

History:

Wisdom:

Prophets:

Gospels:

Letters:

Biblical Theological Theme:

Definition:

Major Developments, Typology, Fulfillment:

Relevance and Application:

Books, Resources, Reference Material:

Metanarrative Developments and Exegetical Analysis:

Pentateuch:

History:

Wisdom:

Prophets:

Gospels:

Letters:

Biblical Theological Theme:

Definition:

Major Developments, Typology, Fulfillment:

Relevance and Application:

Books, Resources, Reference Material:

Metanarrative Developments and Exegetical Analysis:

Pentateuch:

History:

Wisdom:

Prophets:

Gospels:

Letters:

Biblical Theological Theme:

Definition:

Major Developments, Typology, Fulfillment:

Relevance and Application:

Books, Resources, Reference Material:

Metanarrative Developments and Exegetical Analysis:

Pentateuch:

History:

Wisdom:

Prophets:

Gospels:

Letters:

Biblical Theological Theme:

Definition:

Major Developments, Typology, Fulfillment:

Relevance and Application:

Books, Resources, Reference Material:

Metanarrative Developments and Exegetical Analysis:

Pentateuch:

History:

Wisdom:

Prophets:

Gospels:

Letters:

Biblical Theological Theme:

Definition:

Major Developments, Typology, Fulfillment:

Relevance and Application:

Books, Resources, Reference Material:

Metanarrative Developments and Exegetical Analysis:

Pentateuch:

History:

Wisdom:

Prophets:

Gospels:

Letters:

Biblical Theological Theme:

Definition:

Major Developments, Typology, Fulfillment:

Relevance and Application:

Books, Resources, Reference Material:

Metanarrative Developments and Exegetical Analysis:

Pentateuch:

History:

Wisdom:

Prophets:

Gospels:

Letters:

Biblical Theological Theme:

Definition:

Major Developments, Typology, Fulfillment:

Relevance and Application:

Books, Resources, Reference Material:

Metanarrative Developments and Exegetical Analysis:

Pentateuch:

History:

Wisdom:

Prophets:

Gospels:

Letters:

APPENDIX A

This Appendix is a short list of themes to give you a springboard into thinking biblical-theologically. This list is nowhere near exhaustive.

Covenants
Knowing God
Presence of God
Kingdom
Sonship
Image of God
Mission
Prayer
Work of the Spirit
New Creation
Glory
Sabbath
Sin
Justice
Hope
Redemption
Environment
Hospitality
Pastors/Shepherds
Leadership
The People of God
The Exodus
Passover

Priesthood
Death
Wisdom
Slavery/Devotion
Possessions
Land
Temple
Holiness
Spiritual Adultery
Sexual Violence
Thanksgiving
Trinity
Identity
Obedience
Commandments
Heaven/Hell
Repentance
Torah
Divine Counsel
Adam
David
Abraham
Resurrection

APPENDIX B

LIST OF BIBLICAL THEOLOGICAL INTRODUCTIONS

Alexander, Carson, Goldsworthy, Rosner, *New Dictionary of Biblical Theology* (IVPress, 2000).

Beale, G. K., and Benjamin Gladd, *The Story Retold* (IVPress, 2020).

Goldsworthy, Graeme, *Christ-Centered Biblical Theology* (IVP Academic, 2012).

Goldsworthy, Graeme, *Preaching the Whole Bible as Christian Scripture: The Application of Biblical Theology to Expository Preaching* (Eerdmans, 2000).

Hamilton Jr., James M., *What is Biblical Theology?* (Crossway, 2013).

Klink III, Edward W. and Darian R. Lockett, *Understanding Biblical Theology: A Comparison of Theory and Practice* (Zondervan Academic, 2012). (My Biblical Theology Profs!)

Kruger, Michael J., et al., *A Biblical-Theological Introduction to the New Testament* (Crossway, 2016).

Lawrence, Michael, *Biblical Theology in the Life of the Church,* (9Marks, 2010).

Roark, Nick and Robert Cline, *Biblical Theology* (Crossway, 2018).

Van Pelt, Miles, et al., *A Biblical-Theological Introduction to the Old Testament* (Crossway, 2016).

Vos, Geerhardus, *Biblical Theology,* (Banner of Truth, 2014).

APPENDIX C

As detailed in the introduction of this workbook, I delineate between two different approaches to Biblical Theology. First, there's the 'Centric' approach that seeks to discover the *central* theme that upholds the biblical narrative. Second, the 'Thematic' approach takes the various themes found in Scripture and follows them through the canon without arguing for their centrality.

Centric Approaches

Beale, GK, *A New Testament Biblical Theology* (Baker Academic, 2011).

Bruno, Chris, *The Whole Message of the Bible in 16 Words* (Crossway, 2017).

Hafemann, and House, *Central Themes in Biblical Theology* (IVPress, 2007).

Hamilton Jr., James M, *God's Glory in Salvation through Judgment* (Crossway, 2010).

Schreiner, Tom, *The King in His Beauty: A Biblical Theology of the Old and New Testaments* (Baker Academic, 2013).

Wellum, Stephen and Peter Gentry, *Kingdom Through Covenant*, 2nd ed. (Crossway, 2018)

Thematic Approaches

Series:
New Studies in Biblical Theology (IVPress)
There are currently 48 volumes in this series all dealing with different biblical-theological themes. These are among the best resources for thematic studies.

Short Studies in Biblical Theology (Crossway)
There are currently 11 volumes in this series dealing with different themes. These are short, accessible, and incredible potent volumes to glean from.

Essential Studies in Biblical Theology (IVPress)
This is a newer series that consists of 2 volumes currently, but is one of the most promising series of books I've seen. Benjamin Gladd is the editor and the first two volumes are incredible.

Standalone:
Ash, Christopher, *Remaking a Broken World* (The Good Book Company, 2019).

Beale, G. K., *God Dwells Among Us* (IVP Books, 2014).

Beale, G. K., *We Become What We Worship* (IVPress, 2008).

Beale, G. K., and Benjamin Gladd, *Hidden but Now Revealed* (IVP Academic, 2014).

Childs, Brevard S., *Biblical Theology of the Old and New Testaments* (Augsburg Fortress Publishing, 2011).

Estelle, Brian D., *Echoes of Exodus* (IVPress, 2018).

Goldingay, John, *Biblical Theology* (IVP Academic, 2016).

Goldsworthy, Graeme, *According to Plan* (IVP Academic, 2002).

Imes, Carmen Joy, *Bearing God's Name* (IVPress, 2019).

Roberts, Vaughn, *God's Big Picture* (IVP Books, 2003).

Witherington III, Ben, *Biblical Theology* (Cambridge University Press, 2019).

Printed in Great Britain
by Amazon

35591067R00095